The Ultimate Michigan Car Accident Handbook

A Practical Guide to Understanding Your Legal Rights!

The Ultimate Michigan Car Accident Handbook

A Practical Guide to Understanding Your Legal Rights!

Lawrence J. Buckfire, Attorney

WORD ASSOCIATION PUBLISHERS
www.wordassociation.com
1.800.827.7903

Printed in the United States of America

ISBN: 978-1-55971-223-3

Designed and published by

Word Association Publishers
205 Fifth Avenue
Tarentum , Pennsylvania 15084

www.wordassociation.com
1.800.827.7903

Contents

Who I Am and Why I Wrote This Book

I am attorney Lawrence J. Buckfire and I am the owner at the law firm of Buckfire & Buckfire, P.C. I have an undergraduate degree in economics from the University of Michigan and a juris doctor degree from Wayne State University School of Law.

I am recognized as an expert in cases involving auto accident injury cases and auto insurance laws. I am frequently asked to speak to groups of other lawyers on these topics and am often contacted by medical professionals who have questions on behalf of their patients who have been injured in accidents.

I wrote this book to help you understand your legal rights if you were injured in a car accident. The insurance laws in Michigan that apply to car accidents are very complicated and change on almost a daily basis. This book was written to make these laws easy to understand to someone who is not a lawyer or a judge.

This book may not answer all of your questions and simply cannot cover every aspect of the Michigan No-Fault insurance law. I am very proud to say that I have helped hundreds of injured clients, just like you, with their cases in the last seventeen years. To learn more about my record of success, please visit our firm web site for some examples of the settlements and jury verdicts that were obtained for my clients.

I always look forward to sharing my expertise with new clients and gladly speak with all persons who call my office. If you know others who would benefit from this book, please have them call me and I will send them a complimentary copy.

Lawrence J. Buckfire, Attorney at Law
larry@buckfirelaw.com
Specializing in Auto Accident and Insurance Claims
www.buckfirelaw.com
Toll-Free: (800) 606-1717

Legal Advice

I am not allowed to give legal advice in this book and you should not take the information in the book as legal advice. It is intended to be informative and to provide you and your family with a basic understanding of your rights. If you hire my firm to represent you or a family member for a case, I will fully explain your legal rights under Michigan law to you and assist you in filing your claims. If you have already hired a lawyer before reading this book, you should contact your lawyer with specific questions about your legal rights and benefits.

Choosing The Right Lawyer For Your Case

Do all lawyers in Michigan know how to handle auto accident and injury cases?

No. The insurance laws in Michigan regarding motor vehicle accidents are very confusing and change on a daily basis. The No-Fault law was created in 1973 and there have been over 2,000 written court opinions regarding these laws.

The fact that Attorney Ernie drafted a will for your uncle or that Lawyer Linda handled your cousin's divorce case does not make them qualified to handle an auto accident case. Many attorneys who claim to be specialists in auto accident cases do not know the intricacies of these laws.

While many lawyers will offer to represent you in your case, it is important to choose a lawyer who handles serious motor vehicle accident injury cases everyday and has significant experience and expertise in representing injury victims. Lawyers without this knowledge and experience may not be familiar with or even understand these laws and its many technicalities—shortcomings which could cause you to lose your benefits and your opportunity to obtain a settlement.

How do you find the best lawyer for your case?

The best way to find the right lawyer is to know the right questions to ask a lawyer before you hire a lawyer for your case. These questions are a good start:

1. What percentage of your practice is devoted to handling serious auto accident injury claims?

2. Have you ever written a book, like this one, on auto accidents and insurance claims?

3. Have you ever spoken to groups of other lawyers and professionals about auto accident cases and auto insurance laws?

4. Do you have a website with information on auto accident cases and free forms that I can print to make my insurance claims?

5. Have you ever taken an auto accident case to trial and won a verdict for your client?

6. What kinds of settlements have you received for your clients?

The lawyers at **Buckfire & Buckfire P.C.** will give you direct answers to these questions. Our firm has represented auto accident injury victims and their families throughout the State of Michigan for almost 40 years. Our lawyers have the knowledge, expertise, and experience in handling these cases. Most of our clients are referred to us from other clients, who have placed their trust in us to represent their family members, friends, and colleagues. We also receive many referrals from other lawyers and from medical professionals, who recognize that we are the best law firm to represent their clients and patients.

What does the phrase "No-Fault" mean anyways?

Most of you have heard the phrase "No-Fault" but do not know exactly what it means or how it affects you if you are involved in a car accident. You are not alone.

Basically, it means that you can get insurance benefits regardless of whether you or someone else was at fault in the accident. **That's right, you are entitled to insurance benefits even if you were at fault in the accident.**

Generally, when you are involved in a car accident in Michigan, there are three types of insurance claims. These claims are explained in more detail in this book, but they are classified as:

1. Car Repairs and Damages
(Payment for repairs to your vehicle)

2. Bodily Injury Claims
(Payment for your personal injuries)

3. No-Fault Insurance Benefits
(Payment for wage loss, medical expenses, etc.)

Because Michigan is a no-fault state, you are required to make claims against your own insurance company for car repairs and no-fault benefits. Michigan law also allows you to make a claim against the driver and owner of the car who was at fault in the accident if you suffered personal injuries, such as for pain and suffering and any visible scars or disfigurement. These are called bodily injury claims.

In this book, I will tell you how to make these claims and will answer many of your common questions. Of course, if you have questions that are not answered in this book, you can always pick up the telephone and give me a call. My toll-free number is 1-800-606-1717.

Car Repairs and Damage Claims

Who has to pay for the repairs and damages to my car?

How much you will receive depends on whether you or the other driver was at fault and on what type of collision coverage you had on the car. Your own car insurance pays for the repairs on your vehicle.

What types of collision coverage are there?

There are three types of collision coverage for repairs to your car. They are called Limited Collision Coverage, Standard Collision Coverage, and Broad Form Collision Coverage.

What if I did not buy collision coverage?

If you did not buy collision coverage, you will have to pay for the repairs to your car even if you were not at fault in the accident. You may be able to recover up to $500.00 from the other driver or his insurance company. This is called a mini-tort claim.

What is a deductible?

This is the amount that you agree to pay toward the cost of repairs before the insurance company steps in to pay the rest.

How much money out of my pocket will I have to pay for the repairs?

This depends on which type of coverage you had at the time of the accident. Once you have determined whether you have Limited Collision Coverage, Standard Collision Coverage, or Broad Form Collision Coverage, you need to determine who was at fault for the accident. Call your car insurance agent for a further explanation of the type of coverage on your vehicle.

Do I have to pay for repairs and damages to another person's car if I caused the accident?

If you had insurance on your vehicle, the most you will have to pay is the deductible for the other car. The maximum is $500.00. If the other car was not insured for collision coverage, the most you will have to pay is $500.00 even if the damage costs much more to repair. The amount you are required to pay is still based upon your percentage of fault in the accident. Also, many times your insurance policy will cover the other driver's deductible if you were at fault in the accident.

This sounds confusing. How do I know how much I have to pay or my insurance company has to pay?

Accident More than 50% Your Fault

Type of Coverage	Who Pays
Limited Collision Coverage	Your insurance company pays nothing. You pay for all repairs.
Standard Collision Coverage	Your insurance company pays but you must pay your deductible.
Broad Form Collision Coverage	Your insurance company pays but you must pay your deductible.

Accident Less than 50% Your Fault

Type of Coverage	Who Pays
Limited Collision Coverage	Your insurance company pays but you must pay your deductible.
Standard Collision Coverage	Your insurance company pays but you must pay your deductible.
Broad Form Collision Coverage	Your insurance company pays and you do not have to pay your deductible.

I recommend that you consult with a knowledgeable attorney to determine exactly what type of coverage you had and who has to pay for the repairs to your damaged car.

Being Compensated for Your Personal Injuries

I have showed you how to obtain money to have your car repaired. Now I will answer the most common questions asked about how to receive a settlement for your injuries.

If I was driving a car or was a passenger in a car that was struck by another car, can I sue the driver and the owner of the car that caused the accident for my injuries?

Yes. If the driver of the other car was at fault in the accident and you suffered a serious injury or disfigurement (like a scar), you can sue the driver and the owner of the other car. A claim is made against the driver and owner of the car that caused the accident, and your damages are covered by their insurance company.

If I was a pedestrian or was riding a bicycle and I was struck by a car, can I sue the driver and owner of that car for my injuries?

Yes. If the driver of the other car was at fault in the accident and you suffered a serious injury or disfigurement (like a scar), you can sue the driver and the owner of the other car. A claim is made against the driver and owner of the car that caused the accident, and your damages are covered by their insurance company.

If I was a passenger in a car and the driver of my car caused the accident, can I sue the driver of my vehicle for my injuries?

Yes. If the driver of the car that you were in was at fault in the accident and you suffered a serious injury or disfigurement (like a scar), you can sue the driver and the owner of the car. A claim is made against the driver and owner of the car that you were in, and your damages are covered by their insurance company.

What if I was a passenger in a car being driven by a friend or family member? Could I still make a claim against their insurance policy?

Yes, if you suffered a serious injury or disfigurement (like a scar), you are still entitled to make a claim against your family member or friend. Remember, your damages are covered by their insurance company.

What injuries are considered serious?

There is no specific injury that automatically qualifies as a "serious" injury and this is determined on a case by case basis. However, here are some examples of injuries that may qualify:

- Fractured and broken bones

- Back and neck injuries, like herniated and bulging discs

- Nerve damage

- Injuries that require surgery or substantial treatment

- Closed head and traumatic brain injuries

- Spinal cord injuries

- Psychological injuries, like depression and post-traumatic stress disorder

- Injuries which cause disability from work and other daily activities

How much time do I have to sue the driver and the owner of the car that caused the accident?

You typically must file a lawsuit with the court within three years of the date of the accident. If the injured person is a child or a person with a mental disability, this period can often be extended beyond three years. In order to protect your rights, I recommend that you contact an attorney immediately to find out the time limitations involved in suing the driver and owner of the car that caused the accident.

What if the driver and owner of the car who caused my injuries did not have auto insurance at the time of the accident?

You may still recover compensation for your personal injuries. This depends on whether you were occupying a car that had **uninsured motorists coverage** or you were covered by your own insurance policy or a family member's insurance policy that had **uninsured motorist coverage** at the time of the accident. This is called an **Uninsured Motorist Claim**. In order to protect your rights, I recommend that you contact an attorney immediately to find out the time limitations involved in making an **Uninsured Motorist Claim**, as well as the requirements under the policy that you must meet in order to make such a claim.

What if the driver and the owner of the car that caused my injuries had only minimum coverage for bodily injuries caused in the accident?

This depends on whether you were occupying a car which had **underinsured motorists coverage** or you were covered by your own insurance policy or a family member's insurance policy which had **underinsured motorists coverage** at the time of the accident. If you are eligible for this coverage, you can often make a claim against the policy to receive a settlement that is higher than the at-fault driver's insurance coverage. This is called an **Underinsured Motorist Claim**.

In order to protect your rights, I recommend that you contact an attorney immediately to find out the time limitations involved in making an **Underinsured Motorist Claim**, as well the requirements under the policy which you must meet in order to make such a claim.

If a family member died from an auto accident, what kind of claims can family members make against the driver and owner of the car that caused the death?

This is called a **Wrongful Death Case** and can be brought by the personal representative of the estate, usually a family member. The claim can be made against the driver and owner of the car that caused the accident. If the other driver or owner of the car did not have insurance, an Uninsured Motorist Claim can be filed if this coverage exists.

Family members of the decedent can sue for the loss of companionship, loss of services, loss of income, and other losses. Typically, the settlement is shared by members of the family and the amount of each share is either agreed upon by the family members or decided by the judge.

What if the driver that caused the accident was drunk at the time of the accident?

In this circumstance, you can sue the driver and often you can sue the place of business that sold or provided the alcohol to the drunk driver. The time frame for notifying the provider of the alcohol of a potential claim is much shorter than the time for filing a lawsuit. In claims involving drunk drivers, it is important to hire a lawyer immediately to start the investigation and to find out where and when the alcohol was furnished to the drunk driver.

Do I need a lawyer to represent me in these types of cases?

The simple answer is "no," but you need to be careful not to sign away your legal rights with the other insurance company for a small settlement. If you agree to a settlement and sign the release papers, you cannot change your mind or come back for another settlement at a later date. It is important to have an attorney review all of the papers before you sign them and assist you in obtaining the best settlement.

Also, there are strict time limitations involved in making these types of claims. It is important to find out those time limitations. Although you may attempt to settle a claim on your own, studies have shown that injured persons usually receive a greater recovery when they have an attorney, even after paying the attorney fees and costs.

How much money can I sue the driver and owner of the car for that caused the accident and injured me?

There is no limit on the amount of money you can ask as compensation for your injuries. This depends on the seriousness of your injuries, whether you can prove that the other driver caused the accident, and often the amount of the insurance policy.

How do I know that I am receiving a fair settlement from the insurance company?

Unless you understand how experienced lawyers and insurance companies determine the fair amount of a settlement, you might have a difficult time knowing whether you are receiving a fair settlement. The settlement amount depends on a variety of factors and it is difficult to know if you are being fairly compensated, unless you know the law and have negotiated these types of claims in the past.

Do I have to go to court to receive a settlement for my injuries?

Although every case is different, most cases are settled with the insurance company before going to court. Sometimes, claims are settled with the insurance company even before a lawsuit is filed with the court.

No-Fault Insurance Benefits

What are No-Fault Insurance Benefits?

No-Fault insurance benefits are benefits you are entitled to receive under Michigan law, regardless of fault, if you were injured in an automobile accident. These benefits include wage loss benefits for the first three years after the accident, assistance with household chores for the first three years after the accident, unlimited lifetime medical expense coverage, mileage to and from doctor appointments, attendant care and other benefits, such as home and vehicle modifications.

What types of accidents will allow me to obtain No-Fault Insurance Benefits?

The most typical situation is when you are injured in a car crash while driving a car or as a passenger in a car, or if you were hit by a car while walking or riding a bicycle.

You may also obtain No-Fault Insurance Benefits if you are injured while entering or exiting a car. In some situations, you can obtain these benefits even if you were injured while loading or unloading your car, such as taking the groceries out of your trunk.

How can I get these benefits?

You can obtain these benefits by filing an Application for No-Fault Benefits with the proper insurance company that has priority for paying your claims.

What if I was injured because I was at fault in causing the accident?

You can receive all eligible benefits, even if you were at fault in the accident. This is true even if you injure another person in the accident, fell asleep at the wheel, or even if you were under the influence of alcohol at the time of the accident. An insurance company cannot deny your benefits even if the accident was your fault.

What if I am a Michigan resident but was injured in an accident in another state? In another country?

If you are a Michigan resident who was driving or was a passenger in a Michigan registered car that has auto insurance or were covered by your own car insurance or a family member's car insurance, and you were involved in an accident in another state or in Canada or Mexico, you are entitled to receive No-Fault Benefits. Also, if that is not the case, many times you still have rights in the state or country in which you were injured, and you should consult with an attorney immediately to determine your rights.

What if I am a resident of another state but was injured in an accident in Michigan?

If your auto insurance company or a family member in your household has car insurance that is certified in Michigan, you may be entitled to receive No-Fault Benefits. In order to find out whether your insurance company is certified in Michigan, you can contact the Michigan Insurance Commissioner or a local Michigan attorney who specializes in car accident cases.

Also, if you were driving or were a passenger in a Michigan registered car that has car insurance, you are entitled to receive No-Fault Benefits.

Finally, if you were a pedestrian or were riding a bicycle and were involved in an accident in Michigan, you are entitled to receive No-Fault Benefits.

How do I know which insurance company to file my claim with?

This can be a complicated question but the No-Fault law sets up a system for determining which insurance company is responsible for paying your benefits. This depends on many factors, such as whether you were a driver, a passenger, a pedestrian, or a motorcyclist at the time of the accident. It also depends on whether you had your own no-fault insurance policy or were living with a relative who had an automobile insurance policy at the time of the accident. Because there are strict time requirements for filing your insurance claim, we suggest that you contact an experienced attorney as soon as possible to determine which insurance company must pay your no-fault benefits.

How do I get my claim for No-Fault Benefits started?

You can obtain these benefits by filing a written Application for No-Fault Benefits with the insurance company that has priority for paying your claims. Your own insurance agent, or the adjuster assigned to your claim, should promptly provide it to you.

We also have the Application for No-Fault Benefits available for you on our law firm website that you can download and print for free. Simply visit www.buckfirelaw.com and look on the Auto Accident/No-Fault Insurance page.

Is there a time limit for filing my claim?

Yes. You must file a written Application for No-Fault Benefits with the proper insurance company that has priority for paying your claims, within one year of the date of the accident. If you fail to do so, you will not be able to obtain No-Fault Benefits.

Also, written claims for wage loss benefits, medical expenses, household services, and other no-fault benefits must be sent to the proper insurance company within one year of the date of the expense. If you fail to do so, you will not be able to obtain recovery or reimbursement for the claim or expense.

Do I need a lawyer to file my claim?

No. You may submit an Application for No-F
your own and submit claims for wage loss bo
expenses, household services, and other no-fault benefits on
your own. Many times, the insurance company will voluntarily
pay the benefits that are owed to you without the assistance of
an attorney.

WARNING: The insurance adjuster may not tell you of all of
the benefits you are entitled to receive from the insurance
company. Furthermore, the insurance adjuster may not pay
the full amount of the benefits that you are entitled to receive
from the insurance company. Therefore, if you are handling
your own claims for No-Fault Benefits, I recommend that you
still consult with an attorney to find out your rights under
Michigan law.

What do I do if the insurance company does not pay benefits?

Due to strict time limitations under Michigan law, I recommend that you consult with an attorney immediately if your
benefits are not being paid by the insurance company.

Is there a time limit for filing a lawsuit?

If the claims are presented within one year but are not paid by
the insurance company within one year of the date of expense
or claim, it will be necessary to start a lawsuit within that one
year period in order to protect your claim. *If you choose to begin*

lawsuit against your insurance company for No-Fault benefits, you must file a lawsuit within ONE YEAR of the date on which the last unpaid No-Fault benefit was incurred.

If you fail to file your lawsuit within this one year period, you will lose the right to have the benefit or expense paid.

If there are any outstanding claims that have not been paid by the insurance company as you are approaching the one year anniversary of your car accident, I recommend that you file a lawsuit prior to the one year anniversary of the accident.

Types of Benefits

Type of Benefit:
Wage and Income Loss

What is it for?

Wage Loss benefits are for your loss of income due to the injuries you suffered in the car accident.

How much can I get?

You are entitled to receive 85% of your gross pay, including overtime, or loss of income, for the first three years following the accident, if you are disabled as a result of the accident.

What if I was self-employed on the date of the accident?

You are still entitled to these benefits if you were self-employed on the date of the accident.

What if I was not employed on the date of the accident?

Many times, you are still entitled to be paid your lost wages even if you were not employed on the date of the accident. If you were a seasonal employee (like a landscaper, summer work crew, or even a ski instructor) at the time of the accident, you can still receive these benefits if the accident happened during your off work season. If you were about to start a new job at the time of the accident, you can still receive these benefits based upon what your income would have been in your new job.

What if I was looking for a job on the date of the accident?

If you were not working but were looking for a job, you are still entitled to be paid wage loss benefits. You will need to show proof that you were trying to find a job, such as submitting resumes or putting in job applications with potential employers. The amount of your wage loss benefits will be based on income from your last job before the car accident.

What if I was being paid in cash for my job?

This does not matter. You simply need proof that you were working and being paid for your work. It will be necessary to file tax returns to show what your income was before the car accident.

How long can I get it for?

You are entitled to these benefits for the first three years after the date of the accident, if you are unable to work. If you are still unable to work after the three year anniversary of your accident, you may have an additional claim for wage loss against the other driver and owner of the car that caused the accident. If you caused the accident, you can only receive this benefit for the three year period.

What if I lost my job due to the injuries from the car accident?

If you lost your job due to injuries from the accident, the insurance company is required to pay your wage loss benefits, even if you are no longer disabled as long as you are trying to find new work after your disability has ended.

What if I can only work part-time due to the injuries from the car accident?

The insurance company is required to pay you the difference between what you were earning before the accident and what you are earning after the accident.

How do I file my claim?

The claim must be submitted to the insurance adjuster assigned to your claim.

What type of documentation do I need?

You need a report from your doctor (usually an Attending Physician's Form) that disables you from working. You also need a Wage Verification Form from your employer to submit to the insurance adjuster. A form for submitting this type of claim can be downloaded and printed for free from www.buck-firelaw.com.

How much time do I have to file my claim?

You should submit your claim for wage loss benefits every thirty days, but claims for wage loss claims must be submitted within one year of the date of your disability.

What do I do if the insurance company refuses to pay these benefits?

If your insurance company refuses to pay these benefits, your only recourse is to file a lawsuit against the insurance company that demands payment for the wage loss benefits.

How much time do you have to file your lawsuit?

If the claims are presented within one year, but are not paid by the insurance company within one year of the date of expense or claim, it will be necessary to start a lawsuit within that one year period in order to protect your claim. *If you choose to begin a lawsuit against your insurance company for No-Fault benefits, you must file a lawsuit within ONE YEAR of the date on which the last unpaid No-Fault benefit was incurred.*

If you fail to file your lawsuit within this one year period, you will lose the right to have the benefit or expense paid.

If there are any outstanding claims that have not been paid by the insurance company as you are approaching the one year anniversary of your car accident, I recommend that you file a lawsuit prior to the one year anniversary of the accident.

Type of Benefit:
Medical Bills, Prescription Costs, and Other Expenses

What is it for?

All medical bills that are reasonable and necessary and related to your car accident are covered by the no-fault insurance company. These medical bills include, but are not limited to, **hospital bills, doctor bills, physical therapy bills, prescriptions, ambulance bills, medical appliances, such as a wheel chair, walker, back brace, etc., and transportation expenses for your medical appointments.**

How much can I get?

There is no limit on the amount of money that the no-fault insurance company must pay for accident related medical treatment. The only limitation is that the medical bills must be reasonable and necessary for your care, recovery, and rehabilitation. For example, a young child who is seriously injured in a car accident may require medical care that costs millions of dollars. The no-fault insurance company is responsible for paying for these bills.

How long can I get them for?

The medical bill coverage is a lifetime benefit. There is no limit on how long this coverage will last. The young child who was seriously injured in the car accident is entitled to receive coverage for his medical bills, related to the car accident, for the rest of his life.

How do I file my claims?

The claim must be submitted to the insurance adjuster assigned to your claim.

What type of documentation do I need?

A written medical bill must be sent to the insurance company. Many times, the insurance company may also request medical records for the bills and also may request that the bills be submitted in a certain format.

How much time do I have to file my claims?

You should submit your claim for medical bills every thirty days, but claims for medical bills must be submitted within one year of the date of the service.

What if I have health insurance? Who is responsible for paying for my bills?

It depends on what type of no-fault coverage you purchased. If your car insurance policy has **coordinated medical**

coverage, your health insurance is responsible for paying your medical bills, and the no-fault insurance company will cover your bills that are not covered by your health insurance, including co-pays and deductibles. For example, if your health insurance policy provides coverage for 20 physical therapy visits per year, and your doctor has recommended that you receive 30 physical therapy visits for treatment for your injuries from the car accident, the no-fault insurance would be required to pay for the ten physical therapy visits not covered by your health insurance.

WARNING: If you are covered by an HMO health insurance policy, and you have coordinated medical coverage in your no-fault car insurance policy, you are required to seek treatment from doctors within your HMO plan. If you seek treatment outside of your HMO plan, the no-fault insurance company may not cover your medical bills.

If your car insurance policy has **uncoordinated medical coverage**, the no-fault insurance company is primary and is required to pay for all of your medical bills, even if you have health insurance. Therefore, if you have this type of coverage, you can see any doctor that you want to, even if the doctor is not part of your health insurance plan.

I STRONGLY RECOMMEND YOU CONSULT WITH AN ATTORNEY IMMEDIATELY AFTER THE ACCIDENT TO REVIEW YOUR CAR INSURANCE POLICY TO SEE WHAT TYPE OF MEDICAL COVERAGE YOU PURCHASED IN YOUR POLICY.

What do I do if the insurance company refuses to pay these benefits?

If your insurance company refuses to pay these benefits, your only recourse is to file a lawsuit against the company that demands payment for the medical bills.

If the claims are presented within one year, but are not paid by the insurance company within one year of the date of expense or claim, it will be necessary to start a lawsuit within that one year period in order to protect your claim. *If you choose to begin a lawsuit against your insurance company for No-Fault benefits, you must file a lawsuit within ONE YEAR of the date on which the last unpaid No-Fault benefit was incurred.*

If you fail to file your lawsuit within this one year period, you will lose the right to have the benefit or expense paid.

If there are any outstanding claims that have not been paid by the insurance company as you are approaching the one year anniversary of your car accident, I recommend that you file a lawsuit prior to the one year anniversary of the accident.

Type of Benefit:
In-Home Nursing Care/Attendant Care

What is it for?

In-home nursing care/attendant care benefits are actually a part of the medical benefits that you are entitled to receive under the No-Fault law and the car insurance policy. These benefits are paid to have a person attend to your personal needs while you recover from your injuries. These services include assisting you with toileting, showering, feeding, and medications, and even just being with you and supervising you during your recovery. The person can be a family member, friend, nurse or someone from a nursing agency.

How much money can I get to pay for nursing care?

The dollar amount paid for these services depends on the level of care and supervision being provided. Ranges are typically from $12.00 per hour to $25.00 per hour. Higher rates are paid in cases involving brain injuries, spinal cord injuries, and other serious injuries that require the most assistance.

How many hours a day can I get it for?

This depends on how many hours a day that your doctor believes that you need these services. In many cases, the rate is paid twenty-four hours a day. Even though you sleep several hours each day, you may still need someone to be home with you in the case of an emergency or even to assist you in going to the bathroom if you wake up in the middle of the night.

How long can I get it for?

Like other medical expense benefits, you can receive this for the rest of your life if it is necessary. Your doctor will tell the insurance company how long you need to have the services provided to you.

How do I file my claim?

A written claim must be submitted to the insurance adjuster assigned to your claim.

What type of documentation do I need?

Again, you need a prescription from your doctor for these services. Additionally, you will need to submit a claim specifying the services being provided, the amount of hours per day the services are being provided, and the name of the person providing the attendant care. A sample form for submitting this type of claim can also be downloaded and printed for free from www.buckfirelaw.com.

How much time do I have to file my claim?

You should send in your claims for attendant care services every thirty days, but claims for attendant care services must be submitted within one year of the date of service.

What do I do if the insurance company refuses to pay these benefits?

If your insurance company refuses to pay these benefits, your only recourse is to file a lawsuit against the insurance company that demands payment for the services.

How much time do I have to file my lawsuit?

If the claims are presented within one year, but are not paid by the insurance company within one year of the date of expense or claim, it will be necessary to start a lawsuit within that one year period in order to protect your claim. *If you choose to begin a lawsuit against your insurance company for No-Fault benefits, you must file a lawsuit within ONE YEAR of the date on which the last unpaid No-Fault benefit was incurred.*

If you fail to file your lawsuit within this one year period, you will lose the right to have the benefit or expense paid.

If there are any outstanding claims that have not been paid by the insurance company as you are approaching the one year anniversary of your car accident, I recommend that you file a lawsuit prior to the one year anniversary of the accident.

Type of Benefit: Household Chores/Replacement Services

What is it for?

Replacement service benefits are payments for services performed around your home that you used to do but cannot do because of injuries from the car accident. These services include but are not limited to cooking, vacuuming, dusting, cleaning, laundry, cutting the grass, shoveling the snow, and even taking out the garbage. The person providing the services can be a family member, friend, or someone that you hire to help you.

How much money can I get to pay for household help?

You can receive up to $20.00 a day for these services. This amounts to $600.00 each month during your recovery.

How long can I get it for?

You are entitled to these benefits for up to the first three years after the date of the accident if you are unable to perform the services yourself.

How do I file my claim?

The claim must be submitted to the insurance adjuster assigned to your claim.

What type of documentation do I need?

Again, you need a prescription from your doctor for these services, a list of the services performed, and the name of the person performing the household chores. A form for submitting this type of claim can be downloaded and printed for free from www.buckfirelaw.com.

How much time do I have to file my claim?

You should submit your claim for replacement services every thirty days, but claims for replacement services must be submitted within one year of the date of the service.

What do I do if the insurance company refuses to pay these benefits?

If your insurance company refuses to pay these benefits, your only recourse is to file a lawsuit against the company that demands payment for the benefits.

How much time do you have to file your lawsuit?

If the claims are presented within one year, but are not paid by the insurance company within one year of the date of expense or claim, it will be necessary to start a lawsuit within that one year period in order to protect your claim. *If you choose to begin a lawsuit against your insurance company for No-Fault benefits, you must file a lawsuit within ONE YEAR of the date on which the last unpaid No-Fault benefit was incurred.*

If you fail to file your lawsuit within this one year period, you will lose the right to have the benefit or expense paid.

If there are any outstanding claims that have not been paid by the insurance company as you are approaching the one year anniversary of your car accident, I recommend that you file a lawsuit prior to the one year anniversary of the accident.

Type of Benefit:
Case Management Services

What are they?

Case Management Services are actually a part of the medical benefits that you are entitled to receive under the No-Fault law and the car insurance policy. Case managers, typically nurses or vocational rehabilitation counselors, play a very important role in helping injured persons with their road to recovery. They often help the patient with:

- Coordinating medical care with multiple doctors and clinics

- Finding the best medical specialists for a patient's needs

- Scheduling doctor's appointments

- Helping the patient with home modifications, such as ramps

- Helping the patient obtain necessary medical appliances, like wheelchairs and hospital beds

- Communicating with the insurance company on behalf of the patient

- Other services to assist the client with their care, recovery, and rehabilitation.

How much money can I receive for case management services?

There is no limit on the amount of case management services that you can receive. The only limitation is that the case management services must be reasonable and necessary for your care, recovery, and rehabilitation.

How long can I get it for?

Like other medical benefits, you can receive this service for the rest of your life if it is necessary.

How do I file my claim?

A written claim must be submitted to the insurance adjuster assigned to your claim.

What type of documentation do I need?

Usually, case managers will send their reports and bills directly to the insurance adjuster.

How much time do I have to file my claim?

You should send in your claims for case management services every thirty days, but claims for case management services must be submitted within one year of the date of service.

What do I do if the insurance company refuses to pay these benefits?

If your insurance company refuses to pay these benefits, your only recourse is to file a lawsuit against the insurance company that demands payment for the services.

How much time do I have to file my lawsuit?

If the claims are presented within one year but are not paid by the insurance company within one year of the date of expense or claim, it will be necessary to start a lawsuit within that one year period in order to protect your claim. *If you choose to begin a lawsuit against your insurance company for No-Fault benefits, you must file a lawsuit within ONE YEAR of the date on which the last unpaid No-Fault benefit was incurred.*

If you fail to file your lawsuit within this one year period, you will lose the right to have the benefit or expense paid.

If there are any outstanding claims that have not been paid by the insurance company as you are approaching the one year anniversary of your car accident, I recommend that you file a lawsuit prior to the one year anniversary of the accident.

Type of Benefit: Home Modifications and Accommodations

What is it for?

Home modification benefits are payable when the injured person cannot comfortably live in his or her current home or apartment because of physical limitations caused by injuries from the accident. The insurance company is required to pay for remodeling for items such as handicapped ramps, additional rooms, wider doorways, and even bathrooms and showers to make it easier for an injured person to live in the home.

How much can I get for home modifications?

The dollar amount paid for these services depends on the type of disability and the special needs of the injured person. Typically, an architect or contractor works alongside the medical provider to design the most appropriate changes for the home. There is no limit on the amount as long as it is reasonable and necessary.

What if I rent an apartment or live with a family member or friend?

You are still entitled to have this remodeling done if you live in an apartment or live with someone else. If you live in an apartment, the insurance company may be required to remodel your apartment or may have to find a better place for you to live that is equipped with accommodations to meet your needs. The insurance company may be required to pay for this residence in full or in part.

How do I file my claim?

The claim must be submitted to the insurance adjuster assigned to your claim.

What type of documentation do I need?

You need a prescription from your doctor or an occupational therapist for these modifications and a reasonable plan for the remodeling. You may need to enter into a contract with a construction company for the needed remodeling.

How much time do I have to file my claim?

You should submit your claim for these expenses once it has been determined by a doctor that it is necessary and you have a contract for the necessary remodeling work.

What do I do if the insurance company refuses to pay these benefits?

If your insurance company refuses to pay these benefits, your only recourse is to file a lawsuit against the company that demands payment for the expenses.

How much time do I have to file my lawsuit?

If the claims are presented within one year, but are not paid by the insurance company within one year of the date of expense or claim, it will be necessary to start a lawsuit within that one year period in order to protect your claim. *If you choose to begin a lawsuit against your insurance company for No-Fault benefits, you must file a lawsuit within ONE YEAR of the date on which the last unpaid No-Fault benefit was incurred.*

If you fail to file your lawsuit within this one year period, you will lose the right to have the benefit or expense paid.

If there are any outstanding claims that have not been paid by the insurance company as you are approaching the one year anniversary of your car accident, I recommend that you file a lawsuit prior to the one year anniversary of the accident.

Type of Benefit: Medical Mileage

What is it for?

This is to reimburse you for your mileage expenses to and from your medical appointments.

How much money can I get?

You are entitled to a reasonable rate per mile.

How long can I get it for?

You are entitled to these benefits as long as you need to get to and from your medical appointments to be treated for the injuries that you suffered in the accident.

How do I file my claim?

The claim must be submitted to the insurance adjuster assigned to your claim.

What type of documentation do I need?

You need to make a list of the days that you attended appointments, the name and address of the doctor or clinic, and the distance to and from your home. A form for submitting this type of claim can be downloaded and printed for free from www.buckfirelaw.com.

How much time do I have to file my claim?

You should submit your claim for mileage expenses every thirty days, but claims for mileage expenses must be submitted within one year of the date of the medical appointment.

What do I do if the insurance company refuses to pay these benefits?

If your insurance company refuses to pay these benefits, your only recourse is to file a lawsuit against the company that demands payment for the expense.

How much time do I have to file my lawsuit?

If the claims are presented within one year, but are not paid by the insurance company within one year of the date of expense or claim, it will be necessary to start a lawsuit within that one *year period in order to protect your claim. If you choose to begin a lawsuit against your insurance company for No-Fault benefits, you must file a lawsuit within ONE YEAR of the date on which the last unpaid No-Fault benefit was incurred.*

If you fail to file your lawsuit within this one year period, you will lose the right to have the benefit or expense paid.

If there are any outstanding claims that have not been paid by the insurance company as you are approaching the one year anniversary of your car accident, I recommend that you file a lawsuit prior to the one year anniversary of the accident.

Type of Benefit: Special Transportation

What is it for?

This is for a van or specially equipped van or vehicle to take you to and from your medical appointments. This is often required for persons in wheelchairs or other equipment that requires special transportation.

How much money can I get?

The insurance company must pay the reasonable cost for this transportation.

How long can I get it for?

You are entitled to these benefits as long as you need to get to and from your medical appointments to be treated for the injuries that you suffered in the accident.

How do I file my claim?

The claim must be submitted to the insurance adjuster assigned to your claim.

What type of documentation do I need?

You need to submit the invoice or bill from the transportation company and a prescription from your doctor for this type of service.

How much time do I have to file my claim?

You should submit your claim for special transportation services every thirty days, but claims for transportation services must be submitted within one year of the date of service.

What do I do if the insurance company refuses to pay these benefits?

If your insurance company refuses to pay these benefits, your only recourse is to file a lawsuit against the company that demands payment for the services.

How much time do I have to file my lawsuit?

If the claims are presented within one year, but are not paid by the insurance company within one year of the date of expense or claim, it will be necessary to start a lawsuit within that one year period in order to protect your claim. *If you choose to begin a lawsuit against your insurance company for No-Fault benefits, you must file a lawsuit within ONE YEAR of the date on which the last unpaid No-Fault benefit was incurred.*

If you fail to file your lawsuit within this one year period, you will lose the right to have the benefit or expense paid.

If there are any outstanding claims that have not been paid by the insurance company as you are approaching the one year anniversary of your car accident, I recommend that you file a lawsuit prior to the one year anniversary of the accident.

Type of Benefit: Survivor's Loss Benefits

What is it for?

If your husband, wife, or a relative who you are dependent upon dies as a result of injuries from a car accident, you may be entitled to receive survivor loss benefits. These benefits include money from the no-fault insurance company for loss of their financial support and loss of household services, as well as payment for a portion of the funeral bill.

How much can I get?

The monthly amount payable for survivor loss benefits changes every year. To find out the maximum monthly amount and how much you can receive in benefits, please call our office at 1-800-606-1717 or visit our website at www.buckfirelaw.com.

How long can I get it for?

You are entitled to receive survivor loss benefits for the first three years following the accident.

How do I file my claim?

The claim must be submitted to the insurance adjuster assigned to your claim.

What type of documentation do I need?

You will be required to submit a copy of the death certificate, as well as a copy of the funeral bill. Additionally, you will be required to present written proof of the loss of financial support and household services.

How much time do I have to file my claim?

You should submit your claim for survivor loss benefits as soon as possible following the accident, but claims for survivor loss benefits must be submitted within one year of the date of the accident.

I STRONGLY RECOMMEND YOU CONSULT WITH AN ATTORNEY IMMEDIATELY AFTER THE ACCIDENT TO REVIEW YOUR CLAIMS FOR SURVIVOR LOSS BENEFITS TO MAKE SURE THAT THE PROPER DOCUMENTS ARE SUBMITTED AND THAT YOU ARE CLAIMING EVERYTHING THAT YOU ARE ENTITLED TO RECEIVE UNDER THE LAW.

What do I do if the insurance company refuses to pay these benefits?

If your insurance company refuses to pay these benefits, your only recourse is to file a lawsuit against the company that demands payment for the survivor loss benefits.

How much time do I have to file my lawsuit?

If the claims are presented within one year, but are not paid by the insurance company within one year of the date of expense or claim, it will be necessary to start a lawsuit within that one year period in order to protect your claim. *If you choose to begin a lawsuit against your insurance company for No-Fault benefits, you must file a lawsuit within ONE YEAR of the date on which the last unpaid No-Fault benefit was incurred.*

If you fail to file your lawsuit within this one year period, you will lose the right to have the benefit or expense paid.

If there are any outstanding claims that have not been paid by the insurance company as you are approaching the one year anniversary of your car accident, I recommend that you file a lawsuit prior to the one year anniversary of the accident.

Free Newsletters from Our Law Firm

Our law firm publishes a legal newsletter on important legal matters that may affect you and your family. The newsletter is very interesting and contains topics that are written specifically for our clients. It is written in the same easy to understand language as this book and it is not the same boring newsletter that you might see from other law firms.

We publish the newsletter four times a year and will gladly send it to you for free and without any obligation whatsoever. To subscribe, simply copy this page and complete the form. You can mail or fax it to us. Fax it to **248-569-6737** or mail it to **Lawrence Buckfire, 25800 Northwestern Highway, Suite 890, Southfield, MI 48075.**

We also send out important legal news updates through e-mail several times a year. We are also happy to send these to you free of charge. If you would like to receive these, please send us an e-mail to info@buckfirelaw.com and we will include you in all future legal updates.

We do not share our mailing list or e-mail lists with anyone else. If you change your mind after you subscribe and no longer wish to receive newsletters or emails, just let us know and we will stop sending them to you.

Please give me a free subscription to your firm newsletter.

Name:_____

Address:_____

City: _____ State:_____ Zip:_____

E-mail Address: _____

Ten Secrets That Your Insurance Company Will Not Tell You About Your No-Fault Benefits

We have written a Free Report that tells you important secrets that your auto insurance company will not tell you about your benefits. Not knowing these secrets can cost you many thousands of dollars in benefits.

We will gladly send you this Free Report if you ask for it. Simply copy this page and mail or fax it to us. Fax it to **248-569-6737** or mail it to **Lawrence Buckfire, 25800 Northwestern Highway, Suite 890, Southfield, MI 48075**.

We do not share our mailing list or e-mail lists with anyone else.

Please send me the **Top Ten Secrets That Your Insurance Company Will Not Tell You About Your No-Fault Benefits**.

Name:_____

Address:_____

City:_____State:_____ Zip:_____

E-mail Address: _____

FREE MICHIGAN AUTO INSURANCE REPORT

Our law firm provides a Free Michigan Auto Insurance Report which can be downloaded online at **www.FreeAutoInsurance Report.com**. The report contains the Inside Secrets to Buying Auto Insurance in Michigan and teaches you everything you must know to fully protect your family in the event of a car accident.

This report teaches you why asking your insurance agent for "full coverage" insurance on your car is not enough. You will learn which insurance coverages are absolutely necessary to have and why you must buy them. This includes uninsured motorist coverage, underinsurance motorist coverage, and uncoordinated medical coverage.

When you request this report, you will also receive the very valuable Michigan Auto Insurance Checklist to use when you meet with your agent to purchase your policy.

We will gladly send you the Auto Insurance Report for free and without any obligation whatsoever. To request this report, simply copy this page and complete the form below. You can either fax your request to **248-569-6737** or mail it to **Lawrence Buckfire, 25800 Northwestern Highway, Suite 890, Southfield, MI 48075**.

Please send me the **Free Michigan Auto Insurance Report**.

Name:_____

Address:_____

City:_____State:_____ Zip:_____

E-mail Address: _____

FREE NO-FAULT INSURANCE FORMS FROM OUR LAW OFFICE

Our law firm provides free no-fault insurance forms on our website – **www.BuckfireLaw.com**. You can submit these forms directly to your insurance company to receive payment for your wage loss benefits, household chores, attendant care claims, and medical mileage claims. These forms include:

- Attending Physicians Report
- Wage Verification Form
- Replacement Services/Household Chores Claim Form
- Mileage Reimbursement Form
- Disability Certificate for Household Services
- Disability Certificate for Nursing Services/Attendant Care
- Household Services Statement
- Attendant Care Claim Form

We will gladly send you the No-Fault Insurance Forms for free and without any obligation whatsoever. To request these forms, simply copy this page and complete the form. You can either fax it to **248-569-6737** or mail it to **Lawrence Buckfire, 25800 Northwestern Highway, Suite 890, Southfield, MI 48075.**

Please send me the **Free No-Fault Insurance Forms**.

Name:_____

Address:_____

City:_____State:_____ Zip:_____

E-mail Address: _____

WA